This Journal Belongs To:

....

Made in the USA
Monee, IL
28 December 2022

23889195R00069